History of Liberia

History of Liberia

John Hanson Thomas McPherson

Olahauski Books

CONTENTS

This paper claims to be scarcely more than a brief sketch. It is an abridgment of a History of Liberia in much greater detail, presented as a dissertation for the degree of Doctor of Philosophy at the Johns Hopkins University. I have devoted the leisure hours of several years to the accumulation of materials, which I hope will prove the basis of a larger work in the future.

J.H.T. McPherson
University of Michigan, June, 1891.

Introduction

There are but few more interesting spots in Africa than the little corner of the west coast occupied by the Republic of Liberia. It has been the scene of a series of experiments absolutely unique in history—experiments from which we are to derive the knowledge upon which we must rely in the solution of the weighty problems connected with the development of a dark continent, and with the civilization of hundreds of millions of the human race. Many questions have arisen which have not been settled to our complete satisfaction. Is the Negro capable of receiving and maintaining a superimposed civilization? Froude declares that "the worst enemies of the blacks are those who persist in pressing upon them an equality which nature has denied them. They may attain it in time if they are fairly treated, but they can attain it only on condition of going through the discipline and experience of hundreds of years, through which the white race had to pass before it was fit for political rights. If they are raised to a position for which they are unqualified, they can only fall back into a state of savagery."[1] Upon the truth or error of this view how much depends! It is shared by many; some even believe that the condition of Liberia tends to confirm it, thinking they discern signs of incipient decay. But the great preponderance of opinion is on the other side. The weight of evidence shows the colonists have at the lowest estimate retained the civilization they took with them.

Many maintain that there has been a sensible advance. A recent traveler describes them as "in mancher Hinsicht schon hypercultivirt."

What might be called a third position is taken by one of the most prominent writers of the race, E.W. Blyden, the widely-known President of Liberia College. The radical difference in race and circumstance must, he thinks, make African civilization essentially different from European: not inferior, but different. The culture which the blacks have acquired, or may attain in further contact with foreign influence, will be used as a point of departure in future intelligent development along lines following the characteristics of the race. This tendency to differentiate he regards as natural and inevitable; it ought to be recognized and encouraged in every way, that the time may be hastened when a great negro civilization, unlike anything we have yet seen, shall prevail in Africa and play its part in the world's history.

If we make allowance for the errors and mistakes of an untrained and inexperienced people, the history of Liberia may be regarded as a demonstration of the capacity of the race for self-government. Upon the capability of individuals is reflected the highest credit. The opportunities for a rounded-out and fully developed culture afforded by the peculiar conditions of life in the Republic produced a number of men who deserve unqualified admiration. From the earliest days of the colony, when Elijah Johnson upheld the courage of the little band in the midst of hostile swarms of savages, to the steadfast statesmanship of Russwurm and the stately diplomacy of Roberts, there have stood forth individuals of a quality and caliber that fill with surprise those who hold the ordinary opinion of the possibilities of the Negro. The trials of the Republic have afforded a crucial test in which many a character has shown true metal. It is not too much to assert that the very highest type of the race has been the product of Liberia.

There are other aspects in which our tropical offspring has for us a vital interest. Perhaps the most important is the connection it will have in the future with what is called the Negro Problem in our own country. There have been and are thoughtful men who see in colonization the only solution of its difficulties. Others ridicule the very suggestion. It is a question into which we do not propose to go. But there is scarcely any doubt that when the development of Liberia is a little more advanced, and when communication with her ports becomes less difficult, and when the population of the United States grows more dense and presses more upon the limits of production, there will be a large voluntary migration of negroes to Africa. And no one will deny that the existence of a flourishing Republic of the black race just across the Atlantic will react powerfully upon all questions relating to our own colored population.

But let us not venture too deeply into this theme. Another claim of Liberia upon the sympathetic interest of the entire people, is that it represents our sole attempt at colonial enterprise. It is true the movement was largely individual, but the effort came from a widespread area of the country; moreover, the part played by the National Government was not only important, but essential. Without its friendly intervention, the plan could never have been carried out. The action carries with it some responsibility. The United States might well exercise some protective care, might now and then extend a helping hand, and let the aggressive Powers of Europe see that Liberia is not friendless, and that encroachment upon her territory will not be tolerated.

A few words upon the topography of the country and upon the aborigines may not be out of place. Liberia is by no means the dreary waste of sand and swamp that some imagine it. The view from the sea has been described as one of unspeakable beauty and grandeur. From the low-lying coast the land rises in a terraced slope—a succession of hills and plateaux as far as the eye can reach, all covered with the dense perennial verdure of the primeval forest. Perhaps the best authority on the natural features of the country is the zoölogist of the Royal Museum of Leyden, J. Büttikofer, who has made Liberia several visits and spent several years in its scientific exploration. The account of his investigations is most interesting. Small as is the area of the country all kinds of soil are represented, and corresponding to this variety is a remarkably rich and varied flora. Amidst this luxuriance is found an unusually large number of products of commercial value. Cotton, indigo, coffee, pepper, the pineapple, gum tree, oil palm, and many others grow wild in abundance, while a little cultivation produces ample crops of rice, corn, potatoes, yams, arrowroot, ginger, and especially sugar, tobacco, and a very superior grade of coffee. The fertility of the soil renders possible the production of almost any crop.

The fauna of the land is scarcely less remarkable in variety and abundance. The larger animals, including domestic cattle and horses, do not thrive on the coast, but are plentiful farther inland. On the Mandingo Plateau, elephants are not uncommon. Buffaloes, leopards, tigers, antelopes, porcupines, the great ant-eater, divers species of monkeys, and numerous other animals are found, besides many varieties of birds.

The native Africans inhabiting this territory are probably more than a million in number, and belong to several different stocks of somewhat varying characteristics. The most common type is of medium size, well formed, coal-black in color and rather good-looking. They are intelligent and easily taught, but are extremely indolent. Their paganism takes the form of gross superstition, as seen in their constant use of gree-gree charms and in their sassa-wood ordeal. Like all the races of Africa, they are polygamists; and as the women manage the farms and do nearly all the work, a man's wealth and importance are often estimated by the number of his wives. Domestic slavery is universal among them, the great majority of slaves being obtained by capture in war. These inter-tribal wars were once almost constant, and their prevention requires the utmost vigilance of the Liberian authorities.

The natives harvest rice and cassada; supply the coasting trader's demand for palm-oil; raise tobacco; procure salt by evaporating sea-water; engage in hunting and fishing. They carry on a number of rude industries such as the manufacture of basket-work, hats, mats, fish-nets; a crude sort of spinning and weaving. Iron ore exists in abundance, and the natives have long known how to smelt it and obtain the metal, from which they manufacture rude weapons, spurs, bits, stirrups and kitchen utensils. The cheapness of imported iron ware has driven out this interesting art on the coast; but in the interior it is still practiced by the Mandingoes, who are also fine goldsmiths, and manufacture highly ornamented rings. There are also silversmiths among the Veys, who do good work. The leather industry, too, has been carried to some perfection.

With all their disadvantages the natives seem to extract a good deal of enjoyment out of existence. They are very fond of singing and dancing to the rude strains of a drum and harp, and usually prolong their revelries far into the night.

Taken as a whole, the native character has many fine traits; and from the civilization and development of this part of her population, Liberia has much to hope.

The Colonization Idea

It is always a most interesting part of historic inquiry to search out the very earliest sources, the first feeble germ of the idea whose development we are investigating. It is difficult to decide from what one origin can be traced the continuous development of the idea which resulted in the birth of Liberia; but toward the close of the last century there arose a number of projects, widely differing in object and detail, which bore more or less directly upon it, each of which may be said to have contributed some special feature to the fully rounded and developed plan.

The earliest of these sprang from the once notorious hot-bed of slavery—Newport, R.I. As early as 1773 the Rev. Samuel Hopkins, then widely known as a theological writer, and responsible for the system termed Hopkinsianism, conceived the idea of a missionary effort in Africa, undertaken by natives properly trained in the United States.[2] This at first did not include the conception of a permanent settlement; but on consultation with the Rev. Ezra Styles, afterward President of Yale, it developed into a definite plan for a colony. The scheme proved popular; it was widely advertised by sermons and circulars both in this and the mother country; and by 1776 funds had been collected, Negro students placed under suitable instruction at Princeton, and success seemed almost assured. The outbreak of the Revolution, however, swept away all the thought of carrying Hopkins' cherished enterprise into execution, and after peace was restored his most strenuous efforts failed to arouse the old interest. Later thinkers, however, found suggestion and encouragement in his labors.

The colony founded at Sierra Leone by English philanthropists drew in part its inspiration from Hopkins' idea, and in turn suggested later American plans. After the celebrated decision of Lord Mansfield in the Somerset case (1772), many slaves escaped to England, where they congregated in the dens of London in helpless poverty and misery. James Ramsay's essay on Slavery soon turned public attention to the Negro, and Dr. Smeathman's letters suggested quite a scheme of colonization. A movement in behalf of the oppressed race asserted itself at the University of Cambridge, in which Clarkson, Wilberforce, Granville Sharp and others took part. As a result of these efforts some four hundred Negroes and sixty whites were landed at Sierra Leone in May, 1787. Disease and disorder were rife, and by 1791 a mere handful survived. The Sierra Leone Company was then incorporated; some 1,200 colonists from the Bahamas and Nova Scotia were taken over, and the settlement in spite of discouraging results was kept up by frequent reinforcements until 1807, when it was made a Government colony and naval station. Its growth in population and commerce has since steadily increased, and it now numbers some 60,000 persons chiefly concentrated in the city of Freetown, and all blacks save one or two hundred.

It may be as well to mention here two other sporadic attempts to lead colored colonists to Africa. In 1787 the gifted and erratic Dr. Wm. Thornton proposed himself to become the leader of a body of Rhode Island and Massachusetts colonists to Western Africa; he appears to have been in communication with Hopkins on the subject a year later, but the effort fell through for want of funds. The other is much later. Paul Cuffee, the son of a well-to-do Massachusetts freedman, had become by his talents and industry a prosperous merchant and ship-owner. Stimulated by the colony at Sierra Leone, and longing to secure liberty to his oppressed race, he determined to transport in his own vessels, and at his own expense, as many as he could of his colored brethren. Accordingly, in 1815, he sailed from Boston with about forty, whom he landed safely at Sierra Leone. He was about to take over on a second voyage a much larger number, when his benevolent designs were interrupted by death.

It will be observed that the colonization plans hitherto unfolded had all been proposed for some missionary or similar benevolent object, and were to be carried out on a small scale and by private means. It is now time to consider one proposed from a widely different standpoint. As a political measure, as a possible remedy for the serious evils arising from slavery and the contact of races, it is not surprising to find Thomas Jefferson suggesting a plan of colonization. The evils of slavery none ever saw more clearly. "The whole commerce between master and slave," he quaintly says, "is a perpetual exercise of the most boisterous passions, the most unremitting despotism on the one part, and degrading submissions on the other. Our children see this and learn to imitate it." And again, "With what execration should the statesman be loaded, who, permitting one-half the citizens thus to trample on the rights of the other, transforms these into despots and those into enemies, destroys the morals of the one part, and the amor patriae of the other.... I tremble for my country when I reflect that God is just."[3] Yet his equally clear perception of the evils sure to result from emancipation immediate and unqualified, makes him look to colonization as the only remedy. "Why not retain and incorporate the blacks into the state?" he asks, "Deep rooted prejudices entertained by the whites, ten thousand recollections by the blacks of the injuries they have sustained; new provocations; the real distinctions which nature has made; and many other circumstances, will divide us into parties and produce convulsions which will probably never end but in the extermination of the one or the other race." After the lapse of a century how prophetic these words sound! Jefferson believed then that by colonization slavery was to be abolished. All slaves born after a certain date were to be free; these should remain with their parents till a given age, after which they should be taught at public expense agriculture and the useful arts. When full-grown they were to be "colonized to such a place as the circumstances of the time should render most proper, sending them out with arms, implements of the household and handicraft arts, pairs of the useful domestic animals, etc.; to declare them a free and independent people, and extend to them our alliance and protection till they have acquired strength."

Such in outline was Jefferson's contribution to the colonization idea. Its influence was unquestionably great: the "Notes on Virginia," privately circulated after 1781, and at length published in 1787, went through eight editions before 1800, and must have been familiar to nearly all of those concerned in the formation of the Colonization Society.

Clearer still must the details of Jefferson's project have been in the minds of the members of the Virginia Legislature in 1800, when, after the outbreak of a dangerous slave conspiracy in Richmond, they met in secret session to consult the common security. The resolution which they reached shows unmistakably Jefferson's influence. With the delicate if somewhat obscure periphrasis in which legislation concerning the Negro was traditionally couched, they enacted: "That the Governor be requested to correspond with the President of the United States on the subject of purchasing lands without the limits of this State whither persons obnoxious to the laws or dangerous to the peace of society may be removed."[4] An interesting correspondence ensued between Monroe, who was then Governor, and Jefferson. Both regarded the idea as something far more important than a mere penal colony. Monroe, too, saw in it a possible remedy for the evils of slavery, and refers to the matter as "one of great delicacy and importance, involving in a peculiar degree the future peace, tranquility, and happiness" of the country. After much discussion Africa was selected as the only appropriate site, and approved by another Act of the Legislature. Jefferson lost no time in attempting to secure land for the colony, but his efforts met with no success. After a discouraging repulse from Sierra Leone, and the failure of several half-hearted attempts to obtain a footing elsewhere, the whole matter was allowed to sink into abeyance. For years a pall of secrecy concealed the scheme from public knowledge.

In the meantime a new private movement toward colonization was started at the North. Samuel J. Mills organized at Williams College, in 1808, for missionary work, an undergraduate society, which was soon transferred to Andover, and resulted in the establishment of the American Bible Society and Board of Foreign Missions. But the topic which engrossed Mills' most enthusiastic attention was the Negro. The desire was to better his condition by founding a colony between the Ohio and the Lakes; or later, when this was seen to be unwise, in Africa. On going to New Jersey to continue his theological studies, Mills succeeded in interesting the Presbyterian clergy of that State in his project. Of this body one of the most prominent members was Dr. Robert Finley. Dr. Finley succeeded in assembling at Princeton the first meeting ever called to consider the project of sending Negro colonists to Africa. Although supported by few save members of the seminary, Dr. Finley felt encouraged to set out for Washington in December, 1816, to attempt the formation of a colonization society.

Earlier in this same year there had been a sudden awakening of Southern interest in colonization. Toward the end of February, Gen. Charles Fenton Mercer accidentally had his attention called to the Secret Journals of the Legislature for the years 1801-5.[5] He had been for six years a member of the House of Delegates, in total ignorance of their existence. He at once investigated and was rewarded with a full knowledge of the Resolutions and ensuing correspondence between Monroe and Jefferson. Mercer's enthusiasm was at once aroused, and he determined to revive the Resolutions at the next meeting of the Legislature. In the meantime, imputing their previous failure to the secrecy which had screened them from public view, he brought the whole project conspicuously into notice. At the next session of the Legislature, in December, resolutions embodying the substance of the secret enactments were passed almost unanimously in both houses. Public attention had been in this way already brought to bear upon the advantages of Colonization when Finley set on foot the formation of a society in Washington. The interest already awakened and the indefatigable efforts of Finley and his friend Col. Charles Marsh, at length succeeded in convening the assembly to which the Colonization Society owes its existence. It was a notable gathering. Henry Clay, in the absence of Bushrod Washington, presided, setting forth in glowing terms the object and aspirations of the meeting. Finley's brother-in-law, Elias B. Caldwell was Secretary, and supplied the leading argument, an elaborate plea, setting forth the expediency of the project and its practicability in regard to territory, expense, and the abundance of willing colonists. The wide benevolent objects to be attained were emphasized. John Randolph of Roanoke, and Robert Wright of Maryland, dwelt upon the desirability of removing the turbulent free-negro element and enhancing the value of property in slaves.[6] Resolutions organizing the Society passed, and committees appointed to draft a Constitution and present a memorial to Congress. At an adjourned meeting a week later the constitution was adopted, and on January 1, 1817, officers were elected.

III

The Colonization Movement

With commendable energy the newly organized Society set about the accomplishment of the task before it. Plans were discussed during the summer, and in November two agents, Samuel J. Mills and Ebenezer Burgess, sailed for Africa to explore the western coast and select a suitable spot. They were cordially received in England by the officers of the African Institution, and by Earl Bathurst, Secretary of State for the Colonies, who provided them with letters to Sierra Leone. Here they arrived in March, 1818, and were hospitably received, every facility being afforded them to prosecute their inquiries, though marked unwillingness to have a foreign colony established in the vicinity was not concealed. Their inspection was carried as far south as Sherbro Island, where they obtained promises from the natives to sell land to the colonists on their arrival with goods to pay for it. In May they embarked on the return voyage. Mills died before reaching home. His colleague made a most favorable report of the locality selected, though, as the event proved, it was a most unfortunate one.

After defraying the expenses of this exploration the Society's treasury was practically empty. It would have been most difficult to raise the large sum necessary to equip and send out a body of emigrants; and the whole enterprise would have languished and perhaps died but for a new impelling force. Monroe, who ever since his correspondence with Jefferson in 1800, had pondered over "the vast and interesting objects" which colonization might accomplish, was now by an interesting chain of circumstances enabled to render essential aid.

Though the importation of slaves had been strictly prohibited by the Act of Congress of March 2, 1807, no provision had been made for the care of the unfortunates smuggled in in defiance of the Statute. They became subject to the laws of the State in which they were landed; and these laws were in some cases so devised that it was profitable for the dealer to land his cargo and incur the penalty. The advertisements of the sale of such a cargo of "recaptured Africans" by the State of Georgia drew the attention of the Society and of Gen. Mercer in particular to this inconsistent and abnormal state of affairs. His profound indignation shows forth in the Second Annual Report of the Society, in which the attention of the public is earnestly drawn to the question; nor did he rest until a bill was introduced into the House of Representatives designed to do away with the evil. This bill became a law on March 3, 1819.

Provision was made for a more stringent suppression of the slave trade: new cruisers were ordered and bounties awarded for captures; but the clause which proved so important to the embryo colony was that dealing with the captured cargoes:

"The President of the United States is hereby authorized to make such regulations and arrangements as he may deem expedient for the safe-keeping, support, and removal beyond the limits of the United States, of all such negroes, mulattoes, or persons of color as may be so delivered and brought within their jurisdiction; and to appoint a proper person or persons residing upon the coast of Africa as agent or agents for receiving the negroes, mulattoes, or persons of color, delivered from on board vessels seized in the prosecution of the slave trade by commanders of the United States armed vessels." The sum of $100,000 was appropriated for carrying out the provisions of the Act. President Monroe determined to construe it as broadly as possible in aid of the project of colonization. After giving Congress, in his message, December 20, 1818, fair notice of his intention, no objection being made, he proceeded to appoint two agents, the Rev. Samuel Bacon, already in the service of the Colonization Society, and John P. Bankson as assistant, and to charter the ship Elizabeth. The agents were instructed to settle on the coast of Africa, with a tacit understanding that the place should be that selected by the Colonization Society; they were to provide accommodations sufficient for three hundred, supplying provisions, clothing, tools, and implements. It is important to note the essential part taken by the Government in the establishment of the colony, for this is often said to be purely the result of private enterprise; the inference tending to free the United States from any responsibility for the protection of its feeble offspring. It is true according to the letter, that the Government agency was separate from the colony: the agents were instructed "to exercise no power founded on the principle of colonization, or other principle than that of performing benevolent offices;" and again, "you are not to connect your agency with the views or plans of the Colonization Society, with which, under the law, the Government of the United States has no concern," Yet as a matter of fact the agency and colony were practically identical; and for years the resources of the Government were employed "to colonize recaptured Africans, to build homes for them, to furnish them with farming utensils, to pay instructors to teach them, to purchase ships for their convenience, to build forts for their protection, to supply them with arms and munitions of war, to enlist troops to guard them, and to employ the army and navy in their defense," These words of one unfriendly to the colony forcibly show the extent to which our national government was responsible for the experiment.

When the Elizabeth was chartered the Society was notified that the Government agency was prepared to transport their first colonists; or more literally "agreed to receive on board such free blacks recommended by the Society as might be required for the purpose of the agency." For the expenses of the expedition $33,000 was placed in the hands of Mr. Bacon. Dr. Samuel A. Crozier was appointed by the Society as its agent and representative; and eighty-six negroes from various states—thirty-three men, eighteen women, and the rest children, were embarked. On the 6th of February, 1820, the Mayflower of Liberia weighed anchor in New York harbor, and, convoyed by the U.S. sloop-of-war Cyane, steered her course toward the shores of Africa. The pilgrims were kindly treated by the authorities at Sierra Leone, where they arrived on the ninth of March; but on proceeding to Sherbro Island they found the natives had reconsidered their promise, and refused to sell them land. While delayed by negotiations the injudicious nature of the site selected was disastrously shown. The low marshy ground and the bad water quickly bred the African fever, which soon carried off all the agents and nearly a fourth of the emigrants. The rest, weakened and disheartened were soon obliged to seek refuge at Sierra Leone.

In March, 1821, a body of twenty-eight new emigrants under charge of J.B. Winn and Ephraim Bacon, reached Freetown in the brig Nautilus. Winn collected as many as he could of the first company, also the stores sent out with them, and settled the people in temporary quarters at Fourah Bay, while Bacon set out to explore the coast anew and secure suitable territory. An elevated fertile and desirable tract was at length discovered between 250 and 300 miles S.E. of Sierra Leone. This was the region of Cape Montserado. It seemed exactly suited to the purposes of the colonists, but the natives refused to sell their land for fear of breaking up the traffic in slaves; and the agent returned discouraged. Winn soon died, and Bacon returned to the United States. In November, Dr. Eli Ayres was sent over as agent, and the U.S. schooner Alligator, commanded by Lieutenant Stockton, was ordered to the coast to assist in obtaining a foothold for the colony. Cape Montserado was again visited; and the address and firmness of Lieutenant Stockton accomplished the purchase of a valuable tract of land.

The cape upon which the settlers proposed to build their first habitations consists of a narrow peninsula or tongue of land formed by the Montserado River, which separates it from the mainland. Just within the mouth of the river lie two small islands, containing together less than three acres. To these, the Plymouth of Liberia, the colonists and their goods were soon transported. But again the fickle natives repented the bargain, and the settlers were long confined to "Perseverance Island," as the spot was aptly named. Space forbids entering on the interesting details of the difficulties they successfully encountered. After a number of thrilling experiences the emigrants, on April 25, 1822, formally took possession of the cape, where they had erected rude houses for themselves; and from this moment we may date the existence of the colony. Their supplies were by this time sadly reduced; the natives were hostile and treacherous; fever had played havoc with the colonists in acclimating; and the incessant downpour of the rainy season had set in. Dr. Ayres became thoroughly discouraged, and proposed to lead them back to Sierra Leone. Then it was that Elijah Johnson, an emigrant from New York, made himself forever famous in Liberian history by declaring that he would never desert the home he had found after two years' weary quest! His firmness decided the wavering colonists; the agents with a few faint-hearted ones sailed off to America; but the majority remained with their heroic Negro leader. The little band, deserted by their appointed protectors, were soon reduced to the most dire distress, and must have perished miserably but for the arrival of unexpected relief. The United States Government had at last gotten hold of some ten liberated Africans, and had a chance to make use of the agency established for them at so great an expense. They were accordingly sent out in the brig Strong under the care of the Rev. Jehudi Ashmun. A quantity of stores and some thirty-seven emigrants sent by the Colonization Society completed the cargo. Ashmun had received no commission as agent for the colony, and expected to return on the Strong; under this impression his wife had accompanied him. But when he found the colonists in so desperate a situation he nobly determined to remain with them at any sacrifice. He visited the native chiefs and found them, under cover of friendly promises, preparing for a deadly assault on the little colony. There was no recourse but to prepare for a vigorous defense. Twenty-seven men were capable of bearing arms; and one brass and five iron fieldpieces, all dismantled and rusty, formed his main hope. Ashmun at once set to work, and with daily drills and unremitting labor in clearing away the forest and throwing up earthworks, succeeded at last in putting the settlement in a reasonable state of defense. It was no easy task. The fatiguing labor, incessant rains, and scanty food predisposed them to the dreaded fever. Ashmun himself was prostrated; his wife sank and died before his eyes; and soon there was but one man in the colony who was not on the sick-list. At length the long-expected assault was made. Just before daybreak on the 11th of November the settlement was approached by a body of over eight hundred African warriors. Stealthily following the pickets as they returned a little too early from their watch, the savages burst upon the colony and with a rush captured the outworks. A desperate conflict ensued, the issue of which hung doubtful until the colonists succeeded in manning their brass field-piece, which was mounted upon a raised platform, and turning it upon the dense ranks of the assailants. The effect at such short range was terrible. "Every shot literally spent its force in a solid mass of living human flesh. Their fire suddenly terminated. A savage yell was raised, ... and the whole host disappeared."[8] The victory had been gained at a cost of four killed and as many seriously wounded. Ammunition was exhausted; food had given out. Another attack, for which the natives were known to be preparing, could scarcely fail to succeed. Before it was made, however, an English captain touched at the cape and generously replenished their stores. On the very next evening, November 30, the savages were seen gathering in large numbers on the cape, and toward morning a desperate attack was made on two sides at once. The lines had been contracted, however, and all the guns manned, and the well-directed fire of the artillery again proved too much for native valor. The savages were repulsed with great loss. The unusual sound of a midnight cannonade attracted the Prince Regent, an English colonial schooner laden with military stores and having on board the celebrated traveler Captain Laing, through whose mediation the natives were brought to agree to a peace most advantageous to the colonists. When the Prince Regent sailed, Midshipman Gordon, with eleven British sailors volunteered to remain, to assist the exhausted colonists and guarantee the truce. His generosity met an ill requital; within a month he had fallen victim to the climate with eight of the brave seamen. Supplies were again running low, when March brought the welcome arrival of the U.S. ship Cyane. Captain R.T. Spence at once turned his whole force to improving the condition of the colonists. Buildings were erected, the dismantled colonial schooner was raised and made sea-worthy, and many invaluable services were rendered, until at length a severe outbreak of the fever among the crew compelled the vessel's withdrawal. It was too late, however, to prevent the loss of forty lives, including the lieutenant, Richard Dashiell, and the surgeon, Dr. Dix.

On the 24th of May, 1823, the brig Oswego arrived with sixty-one new emigrants and a liberal supply of stores and tools, in charge of Dr. Ayres, who, already the representative of the Society, had now been appointed Government Agent and Surgeon. One of the first measures of the new agent was to have the town surveyed and lots distributed among the whole body of colonists. Many of the older settlers found themselves dispossessed of the holdings improved by their labor, and the colony was soon in a ferment of excitement and insurrection. Dr. Ayres, finding his health failing, judiciously betook himself to the United States.

The arrival of the agent had placed Mr. Ashmun in a false position of the most mortifying character. It will be remembered that in sympathy for the distress of the colony he had assumed the position of agent without authority. In the dire necessity of subsequent events he had been compelled to purchase supplies and ammunition in the Society's name. He now found, himself superseded in authority, his services and self-sacrifice unappreciated, his drafts[9] dishonored, his motives distrusted. Nothing could show more strongly his devotion and self-abnegation than his action in the present crisis. Seeing the colony again deserted by the agent and in a state of discontent and confusion, he forgot his wrongs and remained at the helm. Order was soon restored but the seeds of insubordination remained. The arrival of 103 emigrants from Virginia on the Cyrus, in February 1824, added to the difficulty, as the stock of food was so low that the whole colony had to be put on half rations. This necessary measure was regarded by the disaffected as an act of tyranny on Ashmun's part; and when shortly after the complete prostration of his health compelled him to withdraw to the Cape De Verde Islands, the malcontents sent home letters charging him with all sorts of abuse of power, and finally with desertion of his post! The Society in consternation applied to Government for an expedition of investigation, and the Rev. R.R. Gurley, Secretary of the Society, and an enthusiastic advocate of colonization was despatched in June on the U.S. schooner Porpoise. The result of course revealed the probity, integrity and good judgment of Mr. Ashman; and Gurley became thenceforth his warmest admirer. As a preventive of future discontent a Constitution was adopted at Mr. Gurley's suggestion, giving for the first time a definite share in the control of affairs to the colonists themselves. Gurley brought with him the name of the colony—Liberia, and of its settlement on the Cape—Monrovia, which had been adopted by the Society on the suggestion of Mr. Robert Goodloe Harper of Maryland. He returned from his successful mission in August leaving the most cordial relations established throughout the colony.

Gurley's visit seemed to mark the turning of the tide, and a period of great prosperity now began. Relay after relay of industrious emigrants arrived; new land was taken up; successful agriculture removed all danger of future failure of food supply; and a flourishing trade was built up at Monrovia. Friendly relations were formed with the natives, and their children taken for instruction into colonial families and schools. New settlements were formed; churches and schools appeared; an efficient militia was organized; printing presses set up and hospitals erected. On every side rapid progress was made. After years of illustrious service Ashmun retired to his home in New Haven, where he died a few days later, on August 25, 1828. Under Dr. Richard Randall and Dr. Mechlin, who successively filled his post, the prosperity of the colony continued undiminished.

The decade after 1832 is marked by the independent action of different State colonization societies. At first generally organized as tributary to the main body, the State societies now began to form distinct settlements at other points on the coast. The Maryland Society first started an important settlement at Cape Palmas, of which we shall make a special study. Bassa Cove was settled by the joint action of the New York and Pennsylvania Societies; Greenville, on the Sinou river, by emigrants from Mississippi; and the Louisiana Society engaged in a similar enterprise. The separate interests of the different settlements at length began in many cases to engender animosity and bad feeling; the need of general laws and supervision was everywhere apparent; and a movement toward a federal union of the colonies was set on foot. A plan was at length agreed upon by all except Maryland, by which the colonies were united into the "Commonwealth of Liberia," whose government was controlled by a Board of Directors composed of Delegates from the State societies. This board at its first meeting drew up a plan of government, and Thomas Buchanan was appointed first Governor of the Commonwealth, 1837. The advantages of the union were soon apparent. The more aggressive native tribes with whom not a little trouble had been experienced, were made to feel the strength of the union; and many of the smaller head-men voluntarily put themselves under the protection of the Government, agreeing to become citizens, with all their subjects, and submit to its laws. The traffic in slaves all along the coast was checked, inter-tribal warfare prevented, and trial by the sassa-wood ordeal abolished wherever colonial influence extended. Mr. Buchanan was the last white man who exercised authority in Liberia. On his death the Lieutenant-Governor, Joseph Jenkins Roberts, succeeded him. Roberts, who afterward became Liberia's most distinguished citizen, was a Virginia Negro, having been born at Norfolk in 1809, and brought up near Petersburg. He obtained a rudimentary education while running a flat-boat on the James and Appomattox Rivers. In 1829 he went with his widowed mother and younger brothers to Liberia, where he rapidly rose to wealth and distinction. As Governor he evinced an efficient statesmanship that promised well for his future career.

Roberts had not long been governor when trouble arose with the British coast-wise traders that gave rise to a most interesting crisis. The Liberian Government in regulating commerce within its jurisdiction had enacted laws imposing duties on all imported goods. The English traders, accustomed for hundreds of years to unrestricted traffic on this very coast, were indignant at the presumption of the upstart colony, and ignored its regulations. The Government protested, but in vain. And at length the little colonial revenue schooner John Seyes, while attempting to enforce the laws at Edina, was actually seized by the stalwart Britisher and dragged before the Admiralty Court at Sierra Leone. A long discussion which would be profitless to follow in detail, ensued. The result was, that the John Seyes was confiscated. The British Government opened a correspondence with the United States, in which it was ascertained that Liberia was not in political dependence upon them. Whereupon the sovereignty of Liberia was promptly denied, her right to acquire or hold territory questioned, and she was given to understand that the operations of British traders would in future be backed by the British navy.

Evidently if Liberia was to maintain and govern her territory something must be done. The Colonization Society while claiming for Liberia the right to exercise sovereign powers, seems to have had the unacknowledged conviction, that England's position, however ungenerous, was logically unassailable. The supreme authority wielded by the Society, its veto power over legislative action, was undoubtedly inconsistent with the idea of a sovereign state. This is clearly apparent from the fact that though there was pressing necessity for a treaty with England, neither the colony nor the Society had power to negotiate it. It was accordingly determined to surrender all control over the colony; and the "people of the Commonwealth of Liberia" were "advised" by the Society "to undertake the whole work of self-government;" to make the necessary amendments to their Constitution, and to declare their full sovereignty to the world.

The suggestion was adopted in Liberia by popular vote, and a convention met on July 26, 1847, adopted a Declaration of Independence and a new Constitution, closely modelled on the corresponding documents of the United States. In September the Constitution was ratified by vote of the people. Governor Roberts was elected to the office of President, upon which he entered January 3, 1848. His inaugural address is one of remarkable interest, fitly proclaiming to the world a new Republic.

IV

Maryland in Liberia

The widespread interest awakened by the actual establishment of a permanent colony at Monrovia led to the formation of a number of State Colonization Societies, at first purely auxiliary to the central body, but later in some cases independent. The foundation of independent settlements at Bassa Cove and Sinou by the New York, Pennsylvania and Mississippi Societies, and their union in 1837 into the Commonwealth, has been considered. A much more important colony was founded by Maryland at Cape Palmas, which for years maintained its independence.

In 1831, the Maryland State Colonization Society was formed. Active interest in the movement had long been felt in the State, and it scarcely needed the eloquence of Robert Finley, son of the old champion of colonization, who visited Baltimore in that year, to awaken enthusiasm. The Society had hardly been formed when ample funds were provided in an unexpected way. In August, 1831, a tragic Negro uprising took place in Virginia, in which some sixty-five white men, women and children were murdered. The Southampton Massacres were attributed largely to the instigation of the troublesome free-Negro element, and the growing sentiment in favor of emancipation was abruptly checked. The Maryland Legislature, sharing the general excitement, passed in December a resolution which became law in March, and proved to the State Society what the Act of March 3, 1819, was to the main organization.

The connection was more explicit. Three members of the Society were to be appointed Commissioners to remove *all* free Negroes to Liberia. The sum of $20,000 in the current year, and of $10,000 in each succeeding year, for a period of twenty years, was devoted to the purpose. Any free Negro refusing to emigrate was to be summarily ejected from the State by the sheriff. The wave of feeling which dictated this monstrous piece of legislation passed away before any of its harsh provisions were carried out. But the beneficent portion remained in force. The Society was left in the enjoyment of the liberal annuity of $10,000.

In October, 1831, and December, 1832, expeditions were sent out which landed emigrants at Monrovia. The difficulty of arriving at an agreement with the parent Society regarding the rights and status of these people, together with other considerations, led to the adoption of the idea of founding a separate colony. The plan was adopted largely through the support of Mr. John H.B. Latrobe, throughout his life one of the most active and efficient friends of colonization. The motives of the undertaking were distinctly announced to be the gradual extirpation of slavery in Maryland, and the spread of civilization and Christianity in Africa. Cape Palmas, a bold promontory marking the point where the coast makes a sharp bend toward the east, was selected as the new site. Its conspicuous position makes it one of the best known points on the coast, and some identify it with the "West Horn" reached by Hanno, the Carthaginian explorer, twenty-nine days out from Gades. Dr. James Hall, who had gained experience as physician in Monrovia, was placed in charge of the expedition, and the brig Ann, with a small number of emigrants, sailed from Baltimore November 28, 1833. A firm legal basis was projected for the new establishment in a Constitution to which all emigrants were to subscribe. The experience gained by the older colony was put to good use. Regular courts, militia, and public schools were provided for from the first.

The vessel touched at Monrovia, gathered as many recruits as possible from those sent out on the two previous expeditions, and finally anchored at Cape Palmas on February 11, 1834. After the usual tedious "palaver" and bargaining, the natives formally sold the required land. The cape is a promontory some seventy-five feet in height, separated from the mainland, except for a narrow, sandy isthmus. A river, navigable for some miles to small boats, opens opposite it, and forms a safe harbor. A long, salt-water lake extends to the east, parallel to the coast. The land is very fertile and well adapted to farming. Several native villages lie near the cape. From a well-founded fear of native treachery the colonists laid out their town on the promontory, upon the summit of which a brass six-pounder was mounted. Farm lands were laid out on the mainland, and in a short time the little community was in a thriving condition. None of the distressing misfortunes encountered by the colony at Monrovia marred the early history of "Maryland in Liberia."

In 1836 the health of Dr. Hall, whose services to the infant colony had been invaluable, became so much impaired that he was obliged to resign. He returned to the United States, and long rendered the Society efficient service in another capacity. John B. Russwurm, a citizen of Monrovia, and once editor of the Liberia *Herald*, was appointed Governor, and served ably and faithfully until his death in 1851. Early in his administration a convenient form of paper currency, receivable at the Society's store, was introduced, and proved most useful in trade with the natives. In 1841 some slight difficulties with employees of missions led the Society, while still retaining control of affairs, to assert by resolution that the colony was a sovereign State. A revenue law introduced in 1846 soon produced an income of about $1,200. In this year began the trips of the "Liberia Packet," a vessel maintained by a company formed to trade between Baltimore and *Harper*, as the town of the colony was named, in honor of Robert Goodloe Harper. A certain amount of trade was guaranteed and other aid given by the Society. In 1847 the justiciary was separated from the executive; a chief justice and a system of courts were provided for.

The year 1852 ended the period during which the Society drew its annual stipend from the State treasury; but the General Assembly was induced to extend the provisions of the Act of 1831 for a further period of six years. It may be as well to note here that in 1858 a further extension was made for five years, the amount at the same time being reduced to $5,000 per annum.[10] For twenty years the colony had flourished under the care and good management of the Society. Prosperity now seemed secure, and a spirit of discontent, a desire to throw off the yoke and assume autonomy began to prevail. The great success following the assumption of Independence by Liberia in 1847, and the recognition at once obtained from the leading nations of Europe, naturally strengthened the feeling. A committee of leading citizens petitioned the Society to relinquish its authority, at the same time demanding or begging almost everything else in its power to bestow. The Society was further asked by its spoiled fosterling to continue to support schools, provide physicians and medicine, remit debts, and finally, to grant a "loan" of money to meet the expenses of government.[11]

The Board of Managers, though deeming the colony still unripe for independence, generously determined to grant the request, as made advisable by force of circumstances. Among other things it was feared that the better class of colonists might be attracted toward the independent State of Liberia. A sort of federal union with that State was suggested, but found impracticable. A convention met and drafted a Constitution, which was submitted to the Board. An agreement was reached as to the conditions of the transfer of the Society's lands, etc. Both were ratified by the people, and in May, 1854, Wm. A. Prout was elected Governor. Other officials, senators and representatives, were chosen at the same time.

The prosperity of the colony continued under the careful management of Gov. Prout. On his death the Lieutenant-Governor, Wm. S. Drayton, succeeded to his office. It was not long before the "rash and imprudent" conduct of this official precipitated a serious conflict with the natives. An expedition against them resulted in a demoralizing defeat, with loss of artillery and twenty-six valuable lives. In consternation an urgent appeal was sent to Monrovia. The treasury of the Republic was exhausted from the effects of the uprising of the Sinou river tribes; but Dr. Hall was fortunately present, and supplied the Government with a loan from the funds of the Maryland Society. One hundred and fifteen Liberian troops, under command of ex-President Roberts, were soon embarked for Cape Palmas, and easily overawed the native chiefs, who agreed to a fair adjustment of their grievances by treaty, February 26, 1857.

The war was not without important results. The Maryland colonists were thoroughly aroused to the weakness of their isolated position, and determined to have union with Liberia at any price. It was known that the Republic was willing to admit Maryland only as a county, on precisely the same terms as the other three—Montserado, Sinou, and Bassa. State pride and the views of the Society had hitherto kept them from such a union; but now, in the reaction from their recent terror, a vote of the people called for by Act of the Legislature was unanimous in favor of "County Annexation;" and a committee was appointed to arrange matters at once with Roberts. When he declined to assume any such responsibility, they actually proceeded to dissolve the Government, and cede all public property forthwith to the Republic of Liberia. The interesting document entitled the "Act or Petition of Annexation," shows the number of colonists to have been at this time 900 and the aboriginal population about 60,000. The tax on imports produced $1,800 a year. The State's liabilities were $3,000, with assets estimated at $10,000.

The Liberian Legislature by an Act of April, 1857, formally received the colony into the Republic as "Maryland County." The advantages gained by this change undoubtedly more than counterbalanced any loss of independence. Though the total dissolution of the government and surrender of all rights and property before any negotiation with Liberian authorities had taken place, seems inconceivably rash statescraft, the wisdom of the colonists in desiring the union is unquestionable.

At the time of annexation the Maryland Colonization Society had on hand some $6,000, which was invested, and the interest devoted to a school at Cape Palmas; in connection with this trust its existence is prolonged. Up to the end of its period of activity it had received and expended nearly half a million dollars; the balance sheet of December 31, 1857, may be of interest:

State Appropriations, ...,,,.. $ 930.00
State Colonization Tax, ... 12,851.00
Colonial Agency, ... 1,091.85
Columbia Expedition, ... 248.88
Stock of C. & L. Trading Co.... 1,250.00
Mdse., ... 104.62
State Fund, ... 241,922.16
Contributions, ... 45,385.74
Profit and Loss, ... 139,972.31-1/2
J.T.G., Colonial Agent, ... 126.70
——————————
443,883.26-1/2

V

The Republic of Liberia

The History of Liberia from this point on assumes a peculiar interest. The capacity and capabilities of the Negro are subjected to a crucial test. He is left fully freed from the control or influence of an alien race, in possession of a borrowed civilization, and of a borrowed political system of an advanced type, dependent on popular intelligence for its very existence. Can he maintain his position? Will he make further progress, developing along lines peculiar to his race and environment, and spreading a new civilization among the adjacent tribes? Or is he to lapse helplessly back into his original condition—to be absorbed into the dense masses of surrounding barbarism? The question is a vital one. The solution of weighty problems in large part depends upon the answer.

The form of government was, as has been seen, closely copied from that of the United States. There is the same tripartite division—executive, legislative and judicial. The President is elected every two years, on the first Tuesday in May. He is commander-in-chief of the army and navy; makes treaties with the concurrence of two-thirds of the Senate, with whose advice he also appoints all public officers not otherwise provided for by law.

The legislative authority consists of a Senate of two members from each county, elected for four years, and a House of Representatives holding office for two years; four members being apportioned to

Montserado county, three to Bassa, one to each other county, with one additional representative for each 10,000 inhabitants. The judicial power was vested in a Supreme Court with original jurisdiction in all cases affecting ambassadors and consuls and where the Republic is a party, and appellate jurisdiction in all other cases; and in subordinate courts to be established by the Legislature.

The majority of the colonists had been long accustomed to similar institutions in the land of their captivity, and the new machinery of government was soon running smoothly. Within the little State peace and prosperity prevailed; its foreign relations, on the contrary, were involved in the greatest uncertainty. It had indeed severed the leading strings which bound it to its natural protector, and stood forth in the assertion of its independence. But it was wholly unsupported and unrecognized. The dispute with England, whose protegé on the north looked with jealousy and distrust on Liberian policy, remained unsettled. The danger was real and pressing. Clearly recognition must be sought and an international footing obtained without delay. President Roberts accordingly determined to go abroad, and as at once chief magistrate and ambassador appeal to the leading courts of Europe.

His first effort, however, was directed toward obtaining alliance with the United States. In America his reception was enthusiastic. But the delicacy with which the dissension on the slavery question made it necessary to handle every subject remotely bearing on that bone of contention, prevented him from obtaining even the formal recognition of Liberia. Roberts then determined by pleading his country's cause in England to arouse compassion in the heart of the power from which there was most to fear. Here substantial rewards met his efforts. His prepossessing personality, tact, and statesmanlike qualities won many friends.[12] With their support the recognition of Liberia as a sovereign State was soon obtained, together with a commercial treaty which left nothing to be desired. In further evidence of kindly sentiment the English Government presented the young Republic with a trim little cutter of four guns for coast protection. In France and Belgium similar generous treatment was experienced, and Roberts was conveyed home in triumph on the British man-of-war Amazon.

A second visit of Roberts to England, in 1852, four years later, to adjust disputes with traders who claimed certain tracts of land, was equally successful, and France, under Louis Napoleon, presented him with arms and uniforms for the equipment of the Liberian troops. In 1852 Prussia also extended her friendship, soon followed by Brazil and the free Hanse towns. In 1862, the necessity for cautious dealing with the race question having passed away, the United States government at last formally recognized the Republic, and Holland, Sweden, Norway, and Hayti formed treaties in 1864. The consent of Portugal and Denmark in 1865, and of Austria in 1867, brought Liberia into treaty relations with nearly all the leading commercial nations.

The internal condition of the Republic during the first decade was one of unprecedented growth and prosperity. The Colonization Society in America was in a flourishing condition, and gained friends on every side. Its receipts for the ten years were not far short of a million dollars; and this generous means permitted the transportation, in the same period, of over five thousand chosen emigrants. The accession of so large a force of laborers added a new stimulus to the activity awakened by self-government. Many new settlements were formed and all the older ones received an infusion of new strength. Agriculture, especially the cultivation of the great staples, rice, coffee, sugar and cotton, made rapid progress; while commerce was stimulated by the establishment of regular monthly lines of steamers between England and various points on the coast, the first of which was started in 1853. The enterprise of Holland soon added still other lines. Communication with America was at the same time facilitated by the regular trips of a large vessel built for the purpose, the gift to the Society of Mr. John C. Stevens of Maryland.

At the close of his fourth administration President Roberts decided to decline reëlection. For eight years he had been at the helm, and had brought the ship of state safely through her first perilous voyages. And now while the waters seemed smooth and skies serene he thought it best to entrust her guidance to other hands. The election took place in May, 1855, amidst scenes of political strife and party violence at once intense and short-lived. It resulted in the choice of Stephen A. Benson for President and Beverly P. Yates for Vice-President. Both were distinctly the product of Liberian training. Benson was brought over, at the age of six years, by his parents in 1822, and received his entire education in the country. He became a successful merchant and entered political life in the wake of Roberts. As chief magistrate he showed himself a practical and efficient man, with the interests of the country at heart.

One of the leading objects of Benson's policy was the improvement and elevation of the aborigines; but his designs were in part frustrated by the outbreak of a stubborn and exhausting war with the native tribes dwelling about the Sinou River. Details must be omitted for want of space; but this war devastated four settlements and sadly depleted the national treasury. It was soon afterwards that the Maryland colony at Cape Palmas was almost overwhelmed in a similar native uprising, and united with the Republic, as elsewhere narrated.

A widespread scarcity of provisions followed these wars, which gave rise to much apprehension. But this eventually did good in giving new emphasis to the fact that main reliance must be placed upon agriculture rather than trade. The great resources of Liberia were shown at a National Fair, held in December, 1858; premiums were awarded for the best specimens of coffee, arrow-root, cotton, rice, ginger, potatoes, oxen, sheep, swine, turkeys, butter, preserves; cloth and socks of African cotton; boots; soap and candles from palm oil; ploughs, hoes and other implements from native iron and home manufacture; farina; chocolate; planks, shingles, cabinet work, and many other products of Liberian agriculture and industry.

President Benson was reelected without opposition, and entered upon his second term in January, 1858. A fresh outbreak of the slave trade in this year was followed by a number of captures by U.S. cruisers, giving rise to the old difficulty in regard to the disposition of the cargoes.

The Act of March 3, 1819, which had long fallen into disuse, was revived, and a contract made with the Colonization Society to transport and maintain for a twelvemonth the recaptured Africans already on the Government's hands. The substitution of small, swift steamers for the craft of older days so increased the efficiency of the navy that captures were made in rapid succession.

Within two months 1,432 Africans were landed at Key West. This state of affairs made further legislation immediately necessary. Congress, acting upon the suggestion of a Presidential message, passed an Act amending the Act of March 3, 1819, which empowered the President to form a five-years' contract with "any person or persons, society or societies," to receive in Africa and care for the unfortunates rescued from slavers, for the period of one year, and at a price of $100 per capita. Commanders of cruisers were to be instructed to land their captures directly upon the coast of Liberia whenever practicable; immediate measures were to be taken for removing to Africa those already at Key West; and the sum of $250,000 was appropriated to defray expenses.

Three large vessels were at once chartered and stored with $60,000 worth of supplies; with the least possible delay the suffering crowd at Key West was transported to Liberia; but only 893 survived the passage. The effect of the new orders issued to the U.S. slave squadron was soon felt in Liberia. On August 8, 1860, the *Storm King* unexpectedly arrived with a cargo of 619; within twenty-four hours the Erie, prize to the steamer Mohican, followed with 867. Tidings came that still larger numbers were enroute. The effect of this inundation of liberated barbarians upon the small civilized community, already surrounded by savage swarms, may be imagined.

The greatest consternation prevailed, and excitement rose to fever heat. President Benson wrote to the Society that great evils would result unless means were liberally supplied, and entire control of the new arrivals given to the Liberian Government. The Society accordingly transferred the execution of its contracts to that government, and placed at its disposal all money received by their terms. This action seems to have allayed the worst apprehensions; and although over 4,000 recaptured Africans were landed within the space of two months, no harm seems to have resulted. They made rapid progress in civilization, becoming assimilated to and in many cases intermarrying with the colonists; from among them arose some of the best citizens of the Republic.

President Benson's policy in regard to the natives was successful in bringing many tribes much more closely under the influence of the government. A number of steps were taken toward actively spreading among them the arts of civilized life, improving their methods of agriculture, and checking the evils of intertribal warfare and of superstition. A poll tax of one dollar a year was levied on each male adult, to be collected from the chiefs of the several districts; with a part of the funds thus raised schools for popular instruction were to be established throughout the country.

The control and oversight by the central authority of so many small settlements scattered over a large range of coast had been greatly facilitated by the small armed cutter presented in 1848 by the English government. This was now found to be hopelessly out of repair, and was generously replaced by the donor with another and somewhat larger vessel—the Quail, an armed schooner of 123 tons. About the same time the New York Society sent over a small steamer to provide rapid and regular communication between points along the coast. In honor of a liberal benefactor it was called the "Seth Grosvenor."

The third and fourth administrations of Benson passed uneventfully, and in January, 1864, Daniel B. Warner, who, the May previous, had been elected, succeeded him. Warner was born near Baltimore, in 1812, and emigrated in 1823. The Civil War in America, with the sanguine hopes it aroused in the breast of the Negro, caused a rapid falling off in the number of applicants for transportation to Liberia. The income of the Society for once exceeded the demand upon it, and several good investments were made. Liberia, however, was demanding more cultivators.

A supply came from an unexpected quarter. Two societies were organized by thrifty negroes of Barbadoes, to return to Africa and make their home in the new Republic. Agents were sent out, and sympathy with their enterprise enlisted. The Liberian Government issued a proclamation of cordial invitation, and the Legislature appropriated $4,000 to assist the colonists, increasing in their case the allotment of land from ten to twenty-five acres for each family. The Colonization Society devoted $10,000 to their aid, and dispatched an experienced agent to take charge of the expedition. A large vessel was chartered, and after a pleasant voyage of thirty-three days, without the loss of a single life, 346 emigrants were landed at Monrovia. They proved a welcome and valuable acquisition, many being mechanics and skilled laborers.

After the close of the war, the alluring prospect of "ten acres and a mule" having failed our freedmen, the Society again received numerous applications for passage. The M. C. Stevens had been sold during the period of depression; another and larger vessel, the Golconda, was therefore purchased and fitted for an emigrant ship. During her first four voyages she safely carried over 1,684 persons.

In January, 1867, the semi-centennial of the founding of the Colonization Society was celebrated in Washington. From the review of the fifty years' work it appeared that the sum of $2,558,907 had been expended, exclusive of outlay by the Maryland Society, and of the large sums expended by the United States Government. 11,909 emigrants had been sent over, in 147 vessels; of these 4,541 were born free, 344 purchased freedom, and 5,957 were emancipated for the purpose of going to Liberia.[13] Besides these, 1,227 had been settled by the Maryland Society, and 5,722 recaptured Africans had been sent back by the United States Government.

In January, 1868, James S. Payne entered upon the office of President. He is another example of Liberian training. Born in Richmond, Va., in 1819, he was taken before his tenth year to Monrovia by his father. One of the leading purposes of his administration was the establishment of closer intercourse with the great tribes of the interior. These people, the

Mandingoes especially, were much further advanced in civilization than the coast tribes, who formed a barricade between them and Liberia, and offered determined opposition to any attempt to penetrate inland. They feared to lose their advantageous position as middlemen, and succeeded in keeping anything but the vaguest rumors about the interior from reaching the colonists. In 1869 Benjamin Anderson, a young Liberian appointed by the Government, and provided with liberal financial aid by a wealthy citizen of New York, accomplished an extremely interesting journey to a point over 200 miles from the coast.[14]

With great difficulty and the expense of a small fortune in presents to captious and rapacious chiefs, he succeeded in making his way from point to point along a course roughly corresponding to that of the St. Paul's River. The route lay through dense forests, along paths worn by many generations of native feet. The ascent was steady; at 100 miles from the coast the elevation was 1,311 feet, and toward the end of the journey it rose to 2,257 feet. All along the way the population was dense, and showed a steady improvement in character, civilization and hospitality as the coast was left behind. The object of his journey, Musardu, the chief city of the Western Mandingoes, was at length reached, just on the edge of the primeval forest. Beyond lies a vast plateau covered with tall grass, showing here and there a solitary palm, and stretching away to the head waters of the Niger. The climate is wholesome, the air bracing, and the soil fertile.

The city proved large and populous; the houses were small and of a monotonous uniformity, bewilderingly placed without apparent arrangement. The whole was surrounded with a huge mud wall, which served not only as a defense against foes, but to keep out wild beasts, especially elephants, herds of which were frequently seen near the town. The inhabitants were strict Mussulmans, and were much further advanced in civilization than even the most intelligent tribes through which he had passed. They had an extensive commerce with the interior, caravans coming from places as distant as Timbuctoo. Good horses were plentiful, and there were evidences of the existence of valuable gold mines. Anderson was received with profuse hospitality; they appeared to be delighted with the idea of opening trade with Liberia, and promised gold, ivory and various commodities in exchange for European goods.

Another journey with the same general results was subsequently made by another citizen, to Pulaka, about one hundred miles to the southeast of Monrovia. These explorations are of great interest. They show the belt of coast occupied by Liberia to be merely the entrance to a high and healthful interior of great fertility and unlimited resources, over which the Republic has power to expand indefinitely.

President Payne's successor was Edward James Roye, who was duly inaugurated January 3, 1870. Born in Newark, Ohio, in 1815, he had passed through the public schools of his native town, afterwards attending the college at Athens, Ohio, and Oberlin. He went to Liberia in 1846, becoming a prosperous merchant and politician. From 1865 to 1868 he held the post of Chief Justice. Roye came into office at a time when a rage for internal improvements possessed the country; and with this spirit he was in full sympathy. His inaugural outlines a bold and ambitious policy. The resources of the Treasury were entirely inadequate to his extensive projects, and in an evil moment the Legislature passed an Act authorizing the negotiation of a loan of $500,000. The loan was placed in London on terms which netted only £85 per bond of £100, redeemable at par in 15 years and bearing interest at 7 per cent. The amount thus offered was further reduced by the requirement that the first two years' interest should be paid in advance. From the remainder were deducted various agents' commissions and fees, until at length the principal reached Monrovia sadly reduced in amount,—not over $200,000. And this soon disappeared without any visible result. It is an old story; but in Liberia's case it was particularly disastrous. For with her little revenue, rarely exceeding $100,000, it soon became impossible to pay the $35,000 yearly interest on a debt for which she had practically received not a single advantage. And this accumulating at compound interest has reached a magnitude absolutely crushing. So desperate is her financial condition that many believe inevitable the fate which croaking prophets have long foretold, and against which she has struggled bravely—absorption by England.

Serious as were the more remote effects of the financial blunder just considered, its immediate consequences brought upon the country a crisis which might have resulted in civil war. Great dissatisfaction with the negotiation of the loan prevailed. The Administration was severely criticised; serious accusations were brought against it. While the excitement was at fever heat matters were complicated by an attempt of the Administration to prolong its hold of office, which precipitated the threatened outbreak. For some years a Constitutional Amendment had been under consideration, lengthening the term of President and members of the Legislature. The measure had been submitted to the people, and twice voted upon; but the result was a subject of dispute. Roye and his party maintained that it had been duly carried and was a part of the organic law of the land; and that as a consequence his term did not expire until January, 1874. A proclamation was issued forbidding the coming biennial elections to be held.

This action at once aroused violent opposition. A strong party declared that the amendment had not been carried; and in any event could not be construed to apply to the present incumbent. The proclamation was disregarded; the polls opened on the accustomed day; and the veteran Joseph J. Roberts, aptly called the epitome of Liberian history, was elected by large majorities.

Far from being subdued by the decided expression of popular will Roye and his supporters, with the spirit of the decemvirs of old, determined to maintain power at any hazard. Roberts's election was declared illegal, and of no effect. Throughout the summer the two parties stood at daggers drawn. At length the increasing strength of the opposition encouraged the thought of removing the President from office. The legal method of impeachment seemed far too slow and uncertain for the temper of the times. An excited convention was held in Monrovia, October 26, 1871, at which a "Manifesto" was adopted decreeing his deposition. A few extracts disclose its character:

"President Roye has, contrary to the Constitution, proclaimed himself
President for four years, although elected for only two years.

"He has distributed arms and munitions of war, and has not ceased his efforts to procure armed men to crush the liberties of the people.

"He has contracted a foreign loan contrary to the law made and provided; and without an act of appropriation by the Legislature he has with his officers been receiving the proceeds of that loan.

"Every effort to induce him to desist from his unconstitutional course has been unavailing. Threats and entreaties have been alike lost upon him. He has turned a deaf ear to the remonstrances from all the counties of the Republic:

"Therefore, on the 26th day of October in the year of our Lord 1871, and in the twenty-fifth year of the Independence of the Republic, the sovereign people of Liberia did by their resolutions in the city of Monrovia, joined to the resolutions from the other counties of the Republic, depose President E.J. Roye from his high office of President of Liberia; and did decree that the Government shall be provisionally conducted by a Chief Executive Committee of three members, and by the chiefs of Departments until the arrival of the constitutional officer at the seat of Government."

Before the party of the Administration could recover from the shock of this action, President Roye and his Secretaries of State and of the Treasury were arrested and thrown into prison,—a *coup d'état* which made his opponents undisputed masters of the situation. The appointed Committee took charge of affairs; the excitement died away with a rapidity characteristic of Liberian politics, and in January, 1872, Roberts was triumphantly inaugurated. Roye died in prison soon afterward.

A reign of peace and prosperity followed under Roberts, interrupted toward the end of another term, to which he was elected, by a severe war with the Grebo tribe near Cape Palmas. Limited space will prevent detailed consideration of the later history of the Republic. Payne was elected to a second term in 1876. A.W. Gardiner was Chief Executive for three successive terms, from 1878-1884; and H.R.W. Johnson, a native born Liberian, son of the famous pioneer Elijah Johnson, was made President in 1884. The recent years of the Republic have not brought an increased tide of immigration, nor any marked progress. The diminished interest in colonization felt in the United States so crippled the finances of the Society that few immigrants have been sent in the last decade. That large numbers of Negroes are willing, even anxious to go, is shown by the lists of the Society, which has adopted the policy of aiding only those who can pay a part of their passage. Several instances of the formation of societies among the Negroes themselves to provide for their own transportation have occurred. In South Carolina the "Liberia Joint Stock Steamship Company" was formed, which succeeded in purchasing a vessel and sending over one expedition of 274 emigrants. The company was unfortunate and failed financially before another attempt could be made. In Arkansas a large secret Society for the same object was formed, several hundred members of which made their way to New York and prevailed upon the Colonization Society to give them passage.[15]

The culmination of a dispute with Great Britain over the north-western boundary of Liberia is perhaps the most interesting topic of her recent history. The boundaries of the Republic were never very definitely marked out, as her territory grew by gradual settlement and purchase from native chiefs. Even to-day there is no hard and fast interior border line; the country extends back indefinitely from the coast, new land being taken up as settlement proceeds. In 1849 the coast line acquired in this way extended from the San Pedro River on the southeast to Cape Mount, the extreme settlement on the north-west. Between 1849 and 1852 various purchases were made from the natives covering some fifty miles more of the north-western seaboard. These purchases extended to She-Bar, very near Sherbro Island, and were confirmed by formal deeds from chiefs of the local tribes. The conditions of the deeds bound Liberia to establish schools in the districts ceded, and to guarantee the protection, peace and safety of the natives. If now a few settlements had been made in this territory all future trouble would have been avoided; but all available energy was needed for intensive development, and the newly acquired territory was left uncolonized. In the course of time English traders established themselves within this district, who refused to recognize Liberia's jurisdiction, and who smuggled in large quantities of goods in bold defiance of the revenue laws.

As early as 1866 correspondence with the British Government was opened; and Liberia's jurisdiction was more than once virtually recognized. Matters were complicated by the outbreak of disturbances among the natives, in quelling which the Republic was obliged to use military force—a course which resulted in the destruction of property belonging to the English traders. Claims were at once brought against Liberia through the English Government to a large aggregate amount. Holding Liberia liable for damages received in the territory was a practical admission of her jurisdiction. Nothing was accomplished until 1871, when Lord Granville proposed to President Roye, who was then in England, to compromise on the River Solyma as the limit of the Republic. This is about the middle of the disputed territory. Roye weakly agreed, and this agreement is known as the Protocol of 1871. It was not ratified by the Senate. The tact of President Roberts staved off the crisis for some time; but at length the English Foreign Office demanded a settlement, and a commission of two from each State and an arbitrator appointed by the President of the United States met on the ground. Every possible delay and impediment was resorted to by the British commissioners, who further refused to submit the points disputed to the umpire. Of course, no agreement was reached.

The situation remained unchanged until 1882. On March 20 four British men-of-war silently entered the harbor, and Sir A.E. Havelock, Governor of Sierra Leone, came ashore. President Gardiner was intimidated into acceding to the demand that the boundary should be fixed at the Manna River, only fifteen miles from Cape Mount. But when this "Draft Convention," as it was called, came before the Senate for ratification, it was indignantly repudiated. At the next regular meeting of the Legislature in December, a resolution refusing to ratify the Draft Convention was passed, and a copy sent to Havelock. It elicited the reply:—

"Her Majesty's Government cannot in any case recognize any rights on the part of Liberia to any portions of the territories in dispute," followed by the peremptory announcement that "Her Majesty's Government consider that they are relieved from the necessity of delaying any longer to ratify an agreement made by me with the Gallinas, Solyma, and Manna River chiefs on the 30th of March, 1882, whereby they ceded to Her Majesty the coast line of their territories up to the right bank of the Manna River."

Liberia made a last feeble effort. A "Protest" was drawn up and sent to the various powers with whom she stood in treaty relations— of course, without result. The President of the United States replied at once, counselling acquiescence. Nothing else was possible. The Senate authorized the President to accept the terms dictated, and the "Draft Convention" was signed November 11, 1885. On April 26, 1888, Sir Samuel Rowe visited Monrovia and formally exchanged ratifications. Thus once more strength proved triumphant; Liberia's boundary was set at the Manna River, and Sierra Leone, which had possessed but a few hills and swamps, was given a valuable coast line.

VI

Historic Significance of Colonization

Colonization has come to be looked upon with unmerited indifference—with an apathy which its history and achievements surely do not deserve. To some, perhaps the present condition of the Republic seems a discouraging and inadequate return for the life and treasure lavished upon it; for others, hoping for a bloodless and gradual extinction of slavery, the Civil War carried away the chief element of interest. Others still, who looked for a ready solution of the Negro Problem in this country, have gradually lost heart in the face of the increasing millions of the race. And so, some from one cause, some from another, have lost interest in colonization and in Liberia, until a time has come when few have more than the vaguest knowledge of these terms. Sometimes the voice of contempt is heard; but this is always a proof of ignorance. Liberia stands forth historically as the embodiment of a number of ideas, efforts, principles, any one of which ought to secure at the least our respect, if not our sympathy and enthusiasm.

1. *As a Southern Movement toward Emancipation.*

This thesis will doubtless meet with the most strenuous opposition; but a careful and impartial study of the writings and addresses of those most prominent in the movement will convince anyone of their profound hope that colonization would eventually lead to the extinction of slavery in the United States. It must be remembered that at the time of the formation of the Society the pro-slavery feeling in the South was by no means so strong as it became in later years, when the violence of Abolition had fanned it to a white heat. Indeed, during the whole period before 1832 there seems to have been a prevailing sentiment in favor of emancipation—at least throughout Maryland, Virginia, and North Carolina. But the condition of the free blacks was notoriously such that the humane master hesitated to doom his slaves to it by emancipating them. The colonizationist hoped, by offering to the free Negro an attractive home in Africa, to induce conscientious masters everywhere to liberate their slaves, and to give rise to a growing popular sentiment condemning slavery, which would in time result in its extinction. Of course there were those in the Society who would not have subscribed to this doctrine; on the other hand, many held views much more radical. But it is the men who formed and guided the Society, who wielded its influence and secured its success, whose opinions must be regarded as stamping its policy.

The Constitution of the Society did not touch upon this subject. It was needless to give unnecessary alarm or offense. But when in 1833 the Maryland Society adopted its Constitution—a much larger and more explicit one—the attitude taken is boldly announced:

"Whereas the Maryland State Colonization Society desires to hasten as far as they can the period when slavery shall cease to exist in Maryland, and believing that this can best be done by advocating and assisting the cause of colonization as the safest, truest and best auxiliary of freedom under existing circumstances," etc.

It may well be questioned whether such a plan would ever have succeeded: but it must not too hastily be called chimerical. As a practical result it secured the emancipation of several thousand slaves, many of whom were supplied by former owners with money for transportation and establishment in Africa. What further success it might have had was prevented by the rise of the Abolition Movement. The intense pro-slavery feeling which this stirred up in the South caused the Colonization Society to be regarded with distrust and even active hostility. It was accused of secretly undermining slavery and exciting false hopes among the slaves. It was even said to foment discontent and raise dangerous questions for sinister purposes, and was subjected to bitter attack as "disguised Abolitionism."

From the opposite extreme of opinion the Society suffered assault still more violent. William Lloyd Garrison, in his intemperate zeal for "immediate emancipation without expatriation," could see nothing but duplicity and treachery in the motives of its adherents. His "Thoughts on Colonization" hold up the movement to public odium as the sum of all villainies, and in the columns of the *Liberator* no insult or reproach is spared. His wonderful energy and eloquence brought over to his camp a number of the Society's friends, and enabled him in his English campaign to exhibit it in a light so odious that he actually brought back a protest signed by the most eminent anti-slavery men of that country.

Assailed on one side and on the other the Society, as we have seen, serenely pursued its course. Apparently it did not suffer. But it can scarcely be doubted that its growth and expansion were seriously checked by the cross-fire to which it was subjected. Among the negroes themselves prejudices were industriously disseminated, and everything was done to make them believe themselves duped and cheated.

From these reasons colonization never reached the proportions hoped for by those who looked to it for the gradual extinction of slavery. But we should not fail to recognize in the movement an earnest and noble, if too ambitious, effort to solve, without violence or bloodshed, a problem only half disposed of by Lincoln's edict and the Fifteenth Amendment.

2. *As a Check to the Slave-Trade.*

The coast upon which the colony was established had for several hundred years been one of the chief resorts of the slave dealers of the western shores of Africa. Their "factories" were situated at numerous points on both sides of the early settlements. The coast tribes, broken up and demoralized by the traffic, waged ceaseless wars for the sole purpose of obtaining for the trader a supply of his commodity. It was their only means of getting supplies of the products and manufactures of civilization; and, as we have seen, when they found the presence of the newcomers an obstacle to their chief industry, they took up arms to expel them.

Until the year 1807 there was no restriction whatever on the traffic, and the proportions which it reached, the horrors it entailed, are almost incredible. Sir T.F. Buxton estimated on careful calculations that the trade on the western coast resulted in a loss to Africa of 500,000 persons annually. At length the progress of humanity drove England to declare war on the infamous traffic, and her cruisers plied the length of the continent to prevent infractions of her decree. At enormous expense the entire coast was put in a state of blockade.

The result was mortifying. Instead of disappearing, the exportation of slaves was found actually to increase, while the attending horrors were multiplied. Small, swift cutters took the place of the roomy slave-ships of older days, and the victims, hurriedly crowded into slave-decks but a few feet high, suffered ten-fold torments on the middle passage from inadequate supplies of food and water.

The colonists, even in their early feebleness, set their face resolutely against the slave trade: its repression was a cardinal principle. Their first serious wars were waged on its account. Ashmun risked his life in the destruction of the factories at New Cesters and elsewhere. The slavers, warned by many encounters, forsook at first the immediate neighbor-hood of the settlements, and, as the coast line was gradually taken up, abandoned at length, after many a struggle, the entire region. Six hundred miles of the coast was permanently freed from an inhuman and demoralizing traffic that defied every effort of the British naval force. Nor was this all. The natives were reconciled by the introduction of a legitimate commerce which supplied all they had sought from the sale of human beings.

In still another way did the colony exercise a humane influence. Among the natives exists a domestic slavery so cruel and barbarous that the lot of the American plantation Negro seemed paradise in comparison. Life and limb are held of such small value that severe mutilation is the penalty of absurdly slight transgressions, or is imposed at the arbitrary displeasure of the master, while more serious offenses are punished by death in atrocious form: as when the victim is buried alive with stakes driven through his quivering body.[16] The institution is of course a difficult one to uproot. But among the natives in the more thickly settled portions of the country it has ceased, and is mitigated wherever the influence of the Government penetrates, while the number of victims is greatly diminished by the cessation of inter-tribal warfare.

In this way Liberia has proved, from the standpoint of humanity, pre-eminently successful.

3. *As a Step toward the Civilization of Africa.*

George Whitefield is said to have declared to Oglethorpe when lamenting his failure to exclude slavery from Georgia, that he was making a mistake: the Africans were much better off as slaves than in their native barbarism, and would receive a training that would enable them ultimately to return and civilize the land of their nativity. In this bold idea he anticipated one of the leading thoughts of the fathers of colonization, and, perhaps prophesied, a great migration which the world is yet to see. But to confine ourselves to the present and the strictly practical—there is to the interior of Liberia, sweeping away beyond the valley of the Niger, a country of teeming population and vast resources. That this territory be opened to the commerce of the world, and the blessings of civilization be conferred upon the people, it is necessary that some impulse of enlightenment come from without. The casual visit of the trader has been proved by experience to do vastly more harm than good. Vice and demoralization have too often followed in his track. The direction and instruction of European agents accomplish little. The best efforts of all men of this class have resulted in an unequal hand-to-hand fight with the deadly climate, in which no white man can work and live. Besides, the natives need more than guidance; they must have before them the example of a civilized settlement.

It would be impossible to imagine a more ideal agent for accomplishing this work than Liberia. True, its slow development has prevented it as yet from penetrating to the most fruitful portion of the interior district; but so far as it has gone the work has been wonderful. One after another of the native chiefs has sought, with his people, admission to the privileges of citizenship, agreeing to conform to the laws of the country and abolish inconsistent aboriginal customs. The schools are full of native children, while large numbers are distributed in a sort of apprenticeship among Liberian families for training in the arts of civilized life. The English language has become widely known. More remote tribes, while retaining native customs, have entered into agreements or treaties to abstain from war, to keep open roads and routes of commerce, to protect travelers and missionaries and such Liberians as may settle among them. This is in itself an advance; and in addition various forms of knowledge, improved implements and methods of agriculture must enter in and insensibly raise these tribes to a higher plane.

In reclaiming the natives lies a source of great future power for Liberia. When immigration from the United States shall assume such proportions that numbers of interior settlements can be made which shall be radiating centers of civilization, the enormous potential energy of native intelligence and labor will be brought to bear on the development of the country with marvelous results.

4. *As a Missionary Effort.*

The attempts of the Christian Church to evangelize the western districts of Africa constitute one of the saddest and most discouraging records of history. From the first attempt of the Roman church in 1481, it has been one continuous narrative of a futile struggle against disease and death. A whole army of martyrs has gone bravely to its doom leaving no trace of its sacrifice save unmarked and forgotten graves. It has indeed been a bitter experience that has proved this work can be successfully undertaken only by men of African blood, for whom the climate has no terrors. And the superiority of an established Christian community to a few isolated missionary stations requires no demonstration.

From the first the colonists were active in spreading a knowledge of the Gospel among the natives. Lot Cary, one of the earliest emigrants, was an earnest missionary, and besides efficient work at home he established mission stations at Cape Mount and elsewhere.

In 1826 four emissaries of the Basle Missionary College made Monrovia their headquarters, and did some good work; but they soon succumbed to the climate. The American churches of those denominations most largely represented in Liberia—the Episcopal, Presbyterian, Baptist and Methodist—made strenuous efforts, and sent out a succession of missionaries, most of whom fell victims to the fever. Later, after learning the salutary lesson, they accomplished much through the organization and direction of the work of Liberian missionaries. In this way the gospel is safely and successfully propagated among the natives.

A foe more stubborn than paganism is to be met in the ranks of Islam. There seems to be something in its teachings which renders the native a ready convert. Its simplicity is readily understood; and it sanctions the practices of polygamy and slave-holding to which he is accustomed. Under the zealous proselytism of the Mandingoes the Mohammedan faith has taken a strong hold on the interior, and is spreading rapidly to the very doors of Liberia. Candor compels the admission that it brings with it a marked improvement in the condition and intelligence of the converts. Intemperance—which in many cases follows in the tracks of the Christian merchant—disappears. A knowledge of Arabic is soon acquired and the Koran is eagerly read and its principles put in practice. The whole life of the convert is transformed, and he becomes in turn zealous in the dissemination of the faith. The efforts of missionaries alone can never stem this torrent; if any impression is to be made upon the Mohammedan tribes it must be by the extension of Christian settlements and civilization.

5. *As a Refuge to the Negro from the Pressure of Increasing Competition in America.*

It would be unnecessary to bring into review the causes that are operating daily to make the conditions of earning a living in America more difficult. However much or little credence we place in the Malthusian theory of the increase of population, in the doctrine of diminishing returns, or the iron law of wages, all thinking men are agreed that the country is already entering upon a new era. The period of expansion, of the taking up of new territory by the overflowing population of the older districts, is practically ended; future development will be intensive, the country will be more thickly settled, and the sharpness of competition will be immeasurably increased. The possibility of rising in life will be reduced to a minimum; and there will exist a class, as in the older civilizations of Europe, who live, and expect to see their children live, in a subordinate or inferior relation, without the prospect of anything better.

There may be under this new régime a number of occupations in which the Negro, by contentedly accepting a subordinate position, may hold his ground. Or the conditions of life may become so severe that a sharp struggle for existence will leave in possession the race which shall prove fittest to survive. To follow the train of thought would lead into all the unsolved difficulties of the Negro Problem. But surely there will be some among all the millions of the race who will become dissatisfied with their life here. Some will aspire to higher things, some will seek merely a field where their labor will meet an adequate return; many will be moved by self-interest, a few by nobler motives. To all these Liberia eagerly opens her arms. The pressure in America finds an efficient safety-valve in the colonization of Africa.

With such additions to her strength, the resources of Liberia will be brought out and developed. Communication with America will be made easier and cheaper. The toiling masses left behind will have before them the constant example of numbers of their race living in comfort and increasing prosperity under their own government. Many will become eager to secure the same advantages, and gradually a migration will begin that will carry hundreds of thousands from the house of bondage to the promised land.

It is absurd to declaim about "expatriation" and to declare such a movement forced and unnatural. The whole course of history reveals men leaving their homes under pressure of one cause or another, and striking out into new fields. The western course of migration has reached its uttermost limit, and the tide must turn in other directions. One vast and rich continent remains; upon it the eyes of the world are fixed. Already the aggressive Aryan has established himself wherever he can gain a foothold; but the greater part of the country is forever barred to him by a climate which he cannot subdue.

To whom then can this rich territory offer greater inducements than to the colored people of the United States? And what is more natural and rational than that they, when the population of the country approaches the migration point, should follow the line of least resistance and turn their steps to the home of their forefathers.

The sources of information which proved most useful to the writer are:

The Annual Reports of the A.C.S., together with the files of its quarterly journal, the *African Repository*.

Messages of Presidents of Liberia, and the Reports of Secretaries of Treasury, War, and Navy.

The Archives of the Maryland State Colonization Society, preserved by the Maryland Historical Society in Baltimore.

* * * * *

KENNEDY: Colonization Report.

ALEXANDER: History of Colonization. 1845.

GURLEY: Report on Condition of Liberia. 1850.

CARL RITTER: Begründung u. gegenwärtige Zustände der Negerrepublik
Liberia. 1852.

ANDERSON: Narrative of a Journey to Musardu. 1870.

LATROBE: Maryland in Liberia. 1885.

WAUWERMANS: Libéria; Histoire de la Fondation d'un État nègre libre. 1885.

SCHWARTZ: Einiges über das interne Leben der Eingebornen Liberias. Deutsche Kolonialzeitung. 1887.

—Die Neger-Republik Liberia. Das Ausland. 1888.

BLYDEN: Christianity, Islam, and the Negro Race.

BÜTTIKOFER: Reisebilder aus Liberia. 1890.

[Footnote 1: Letter to Philip A. Bruce, dated London, April 8, 1889.]

[Footnote 2: James Ferguson, *Life of Hopkins*. Hopkins' Circular, 1793.]

[Footnote 3: Jefferson, *Notes on Virginia*.]

[Footnote 4: Kennedy's *Report*, p. 160.]

[Footnote 5: A.C.S. Report for 1853, pp. 37-55.]

[Footnote 6: The remarks of these gentlemen and others of similar views have subjected the Society to many unjust attacks. Of course many would join such a movement from mixed motives; but the guiding principles of the Society itself have always been distinctly philanthropic.]

[Footnote 7: Report of Amos Kendall, Fourth Auditor, to the Secretary of the Navy, August, 1830.]

[Footnote 8: Ashmun.]

[Footnote 9: These were eventually paid by the United States Government.
Kendall's Report to Secretary of Navy, December, 1830.]

[Footnote 10: The outbreak of the Civil War ended the arrangement after the third payment.]

[Footnote 11: This singular petition is preserved in Minute Book No. 4 of the M.S. C.S., p. 36.]

[Footnote 12: Carl Ritter, who saw him in 1852, speaks of him as "den edlen, hochgebildeten, erfahrenen, weisen, und der Rede sehr kundigen Staatsman Wir (i.e., Ritter,) haben wiederholt seinen würdenvollen Reden in den ersten Kreisen in London beigewohnt."]

[Footnote 13: *Semi-Centennial Memorial*, p. 190.]

[Footnote 14: B. Anderson, *Narrative of a Journey to Musardu.*]

[Footnote 15: A.C. Reports of 1881 and 1882.]

[Footnote 16: Anderson's *Journey to Musardu.*]

Booker T. Washington: There's no doubt that Booker T. Washington—a former slave who became adviser to multiple presidents—had a huge impact on 19th and early 20th-century politics. Born in 1856, Washington rose to become a leading African American intellectual of the 19th century, founding Tuskegee Normal and Industrial Institute (Now Tuskegee University) in 1881 and the National Negro Business League two decades later. In recent years, Washington has been heavily criticized for encouraging the Blacks of his time to accept the status quo rather than fight for change..

Carter Godwin Woodson: Carter G. Woodson was the second African American to receive a doctorate from Harvard, after W.E.B. Du Bois. Known as the "Father of Black History," Woodson dedicated his career to the field of African American history and lobbied extensively to establish Black History Month as a nationwide institution. Woodson authored several books in his lifetime. In his best-known book, *The Mis-education of the Negro*, Woods contended that the Black people of his day were being culturally indoctrinated, rather than taught, in American schools. This conditioning, he claimed, caused them to become dependent and to seek out inferior places in the greater society rather than rising to their full potential.

Elizabeth Keckley: A former slave who later served as a seamstress, Elizabeth Keckley eventually sewed and became the "personal dresser" for President Abraham Lincoln's wife, Mary Todd Lincoln. Later, Keckley wrote a memoir titled, "Behind the Scenes: Or, Thirty Years a Slave and Four Years in the White House." The book, which told the story of Keckley's time in the White House, was criticized for revealing private information about the Lincolns. In addition to her influence around the White House, Elizabeth Keckley founded the "Contraband Relief Association" that provided resources like food, clothes, and housing to freed slaves.

Frederick Douglass: An escaped slave, Frederick Douglass was an abolitionist, suffragist, and powerful writer whose pen had an enormous impact on African American discourse in the 19th century and beyond. Taught to read by a white woman named Lucretia Auld, Douglass share his knowledge of how to read with other slaves before escaping to freedom in 1838. Douglass is the author of multiple autobiographies including the 1845 bestseller *Narrative of the Life of Frederick Douglass, an American Slave* and 1855's *My Bondage and My Freedom*. Today he is remembered as one of the most powerful voices in the American civil rights movement.

Hannah Crafts: Author of *The Bondwoman's Narrative*, Hanna Crafts was an escaped slave from North Carolina. Although her novel was written in 1853, it wasn't published until this century. The style and content of Craft's novel seems to indicates that she read books (such as Charles Dickens) in the library of her master, since her work bore a resemblance to the writing of Dickens.

Harriet Beecher Stowe: An American writer and philanthropist, Harriet Beecher Stowe authored a novel (Uncle Tom's Cabin) so powerful that it is cited as one of the causes of the American Civil War. Much of Stowe's material for the novel came from the 18 years she lived in Cincinnati, right across the Ohio River from a slave-holding community. During that time, Stowe encountered fugitive slaves and learned about life in the South. She also picked up details from visits to the

South herself. *Uncle Tom's Cabin* was an immediate success, selling more than 300,000 copies the first year. Stowe's classic stoked both abolitionist and pro-slavery sentiment, helping to solidify both sides of the argument. Pro-slavery activists disputed Stowe's account so vehemently that she published a second book the very same year. That book, *A Key to Uncle Tom's Cabin*, documented key details of the disputed parts of her first tome.

Harriet Jacobs: An escaped slave and passionate abolitionist, Harriet Jacobs is best known for *Incidents in the Life of a Slave Girl*, her touching biography. Jacob's book, which was first published under a pseudonym in 1861, was remarkable for many reasons. Named as "the most important slave narrative written by an African American woman," Jacob's classic was one of the first anti-slavery books to address the sexual abuse and harassment suffered by many female slaves.

Harriet Wilson: Though born free, Harriet Wilson became an indentured servant after her parents died. Her groundbreaking novel, *Our Nig*, which was said to have "turned the literary world on its end," was published anonymously. It wasn't until the 1980's, when a scholar discovered Wilson's true identity, that she was credited for her remarkable book. The heartbreaking life story of a black woman in the antebellum North, *Our Nig* centers on the life of Frado, a lively and spirited girl who is overworked and abused by a New England family.

Ida B. Wells: Ida B. Wells was a black journalist and activist who used her pen to bring attention to the post-Civil War lynchings in the United States. Among numerous pieces of investigative journalism, Wells' *Southern Horrors: Lynch Law in All Its Phases* and *The Red Record* exposed many of the cruel and inhuman practices taking place at the time, as well as the political and economic motivations behind them. A former slave, Wells co-owned a newspaper in Memphis and helped to found the NAACP.

James Weldon Johnson: Johnson, who is well-remembered today for authoring *The Autobiography of an Ex-Colored Man*, was a talented poet who also penned numerous poetry collections. A human rights activist and early leader in the NAACP, Johnson extended his influence far beyond the written page by serving as a U.S. consul under President Theodore Roosevelt and teaching literature at Fisk University (a historically Black college).

Jupiter Hammon: Considered to be the first published Black author in America, Jupiter Hammon is believed to have been a slave on Long Island, New York during the 1700's. Hammon's published poems include "An Evening Thought: Salvation by Christ with Penitential Cries," and "An Address to Miss Phillis Wheatley." Hammon is also remembered for his promotion of gradual emancipation and a speech he gave known as the "Address to the Negroes of the State of Ney York." In the 19th century, Hammon's speech was taken up and reprinted by several abolitionist groups.

Lucy Terry: Kidnapped in Africa and enslaved at the age of 4, Terry's freedom was later bought back by her husband-to-be. Terry is the author of "Bars Fight," a poem about a 1746 Native American attack on settlers in Deerfield, Massachusetts. Terry's poem, which was preserved orally until its publication in 1855, is thought to be the oldest known work of literature by an African American.

Mary Prince: A British abolitionist and autobiographer, Mary Prince was born in Bermuda to an enslaved family of African descent. Prince's autobiography, which was first published in 1831, was the first slave narrative written by a woman. An important book, Prince's autobiography provided a powerful impetus to abolitionists and the antislavery movement.

Phillis Wheatley: An acclaimed poet from West Africa, Phillis Wheatley was the first African American to publish a book of poems. After being captured and sold into slavery as a child, Wheatley was taught how to read and write by her captors. Though it happened after her death, Wheatley's poems made an important contribution to the abolition movement.

Sarah Jane Woodson Early: Author of *The Life and Labors of Rev. Jordan W. Early*, Sarah Early was an educator, temperance activist, lecturer and author. A graduate of Oberlin College, Early was the first African American female college instructor. Her book, an intriguing postwar narrative, tells the story of her husband's rise from slavery to become one of the pioneers of Methodism in the West.

Sojourner Truth: An abolitionist and women's rights activist, Sojourner Truth also made several notable contributions to the written word. Though unable to read or write personally, Truth worked with two friends to produce her memoir, a slave narrative which was published in the 1850's under the title *The Narrative of Sojourner Truth: a Northern Slave*. Truth's book, combined with her powerful speech "Ain't I a Woman?" helped shape the dialogue about abolition in her day.

Solomon Northrup: An American abolitionist and the primary author of the memoir *Twelve Years a Slave*, Solomon Northrup was a free-born African American from New York. The son of a freed slave and his free-born wife, Northrup was a farmer, landowner, author, and professional violinist. Northrup's book, which served to educate Americans about slave life in the Deep South, contributed to the growth of anti-slavery sentiment before the Civil War.

W. E. B. Du Bois: One of the first African-Americans to earn a doctorate from Harvard, Dr. Du Bois was an intellectual who helped increase Black political representation. A co-founder of the NAACP, Du Bois has been called "one of the most influential thinkers and activists of the 19[th]and 20[th]centuries." Two of Du Bois' books, *The Souls of Black*

Folk and *Black Reconstruction in America*, are still widely read and appreciated today.

William Still: An African-American abolitionist from Philadelphia, William Still was also a businessman, civil rights activist, conductor for the Underground Railroad, historian, and writer. Before the American Civil War, Still was chairman of the Vigilance Committee of the Pennsylvania Anti-Slavery Society. Today Still is best known for his book *The Underground Railroad*, which documented the stories of slaves who escaped to freedom.

William Wells Brown: A writer, lecturer, abolitionist, and human right activist all rolled into one, William Wells Brown had a great impact on America in the 19th century. In addition to his pioneering work as a travel writer, the escaped slave was an esteemed playwright—the first African American to be published in several genres, in fact. He was also the author of an extensive historical account of Black people during the Revolutionary War.